After Heavy Rains

poems by

Louisa Muniz

Finishing Line Press
Georgetown, Kentucky

After Heavy Rains

ACKNOWLEDGMENTS

I would like to extend gratitude to the editors and publications that first
published these poems (sometimes in earlier versions).

Rose Red Review: Amends, The Droning River
Tinderbox Poetry Journal: A Calla Lily for Maria, The Date, Requiem for a
    Moment Remembered
Snapdragon Journal of Art & Healing: Elegy for the Other Side
Words Dance: Peach Splitting Possibility
Poetry Quarterly: Grief Stopped By Today
The Ravens Perch: The Art of Slicing Cupcakes, Unraveling Knots,
    Grandmother's Fire Dance, A Woman's Shape
Menacing Hedge: Childhood Transformation, Last Time I Buried My Body
    in Silence (nominated for Best of the Net)
PANK: I Don't Tell My Son I Petition Mother Mary
Sheila-Na-Gig: Stone Turned Sand (Contest Winner)
The Magnolia Review: Elegy for a Mother Who Died Alone, Ghosted Album,
    After Heavy Rains, Hunger Song
Jelly Bucket: Silk on My Lap,

Publisher: Leah Huete de Maines
Editor: Christen Kincaid
Cover Art: Photo by Stephen Hocking on Unsplash
Author Photo: Bryan Muniz
Cover Design: Elizabeth Maines McCleavy

Order online: www.finishinglinepress.com
        also available on amazon.com

Author inquiries and mail orders:
Finishing Line Press
P. O. Box 1626
Georgetown, Kentucky 40324
U. S. A.

Table of Contents

Last Time I Buried My Body in Silence.. 1

Peach Splitting Possibility... 2

Requiem for a Moment Remembered 3

The Art of Slicing Cupcakes.. 4

Childhood Transformation 5

Grief Stopped By Today.. 6

A Calla Lily for Maria 7

The Droning River.. 8

I Don't Tell My Son I Petition Mother Mary.................................. 9

Stone Turned Sand 10

Amends.. 11

Grandmother's Fire Dance 12

Ghosted Album... 13

The Date.. 15

Elegy for the Other Side 16

A Woman's Shape 17

Elegy for a Mother Who Died Alone... 18

Pink is Now a Color in the Rainbow 19

After Heavy Rains... 20

Hunger Song 21

The Universe Has My Back 22

Silk On My Lap... 23

Unraveling Knots.. 24

For my mother
Ada Rivera
(1932-2004)

Last Time I Buried My Body in Silence

my emptiness grew teeth.
I buttered the blade of sorrow.

How does a body hold light
in a crushed clay jar?

It's September. The light is supple.
I trundle back to girlhood
a blur of broken shards.

This time Mama came undone.
Perched to jump from a third-floor window.
Ready to tripwire earth.

My body glistens pink,
a hollowed-hum lament
unnamed in throat.

My girlhood bluer than an ocean
weeping bones. Her face turning in light.
Darkness afraid to swallow it.

Mama, don't do it. My gaze
devours hers. Brings her back.
The morning sun mimics wonder.

I am from Mama's spine
where flawed blossoms grow
where flawed weeds thrive.

Peach Splitting Possibility

The boneless tongue is a heartbreaker
it sharpens the blade   by stinging.

I no longer argue.   My heart
is a peach   splitting possibility.

He says I make mountains out of molehills
I'm too sensitive   & I repeat myself.

Who knew trees commune
in the cargo of their roots?

You're right I say & breathe in   fractured air.
I send him white light.

I dream   he's a new lover
tracing my scars. Every day I fail at something.

My intentions too small   a silkworm
unsettled   a stone dragging moss.

I'm whittled down to half human
the other half   carrying me home.

My heart is still a fistful of prickles & sun.
It flowers   in vinegar.

If I repeat myself   it's because
I think I'm repeating myself   better.

Who knew my heart   uprooted tree
would throb in its nest   unheard?

Requiem for a Moment Remembered

I am six and dressed in
a powder pink & blue organza dress,
made by my soon-to-be madrina.
Mami says *it's a special day*
I will be christened & sprinkled holy.

In this moment I pay no mind
to the tiers of crinoline under my dress
scratching legs flogged by a branch,
a tree switch of fire sparking skin,
daddy's way of burning the world.

No one notices me as they prepare for the day.
Don Pocho in the backyard pit roasts the cerdo,
Titi Josefa, hair knotted, stirs the arroz con gandules,
hips moving to the lyrics of Bobby Capo,
Me Importas Tu y Tu playing on the radio.

Daddy, suited up, on the front porch,
sees me & whispers, just this once, aye que bonita.
His words a cocoon of moth-fine thread,
a moment teeming in sunlight.

I watch him out of the corner of my eye.
Songbirds gather in my breath, alight on his smile,
the one I usually see after a shot of Bacardi,
softening his quiet suffering.

I collect this childhood day, save it like a seashell,
lucky stone or rabbit's foot & store it deep,
like a blue jay hoarding acorns.
Deep into the marrow of forgiving.

The Art of Slicing Cupcakes

Third grade—
the year of chalk dust
forever floating past my desk

& Cora, the cupcake girl—
partnered up with me
at a student desk built for two.

Each day her Barbie lunchbox
carried chocolate Hostess cupcakes
in signature lines of white squiggles

& snaking rivulets of vanilla cream.
Bait used to attract her swarm
of classroom honeybees.

Each day at snacktime, Cora deftly used
the pearl-colored cardboard, dividing
the cupcakes down the center.

Afterwards she would name
the classmates she chose to share with.
My heart: a denoted hollow note.

Each day I practiced secretly
words I'd say if selected—
yes, please   I'd love some   thank you.

Instead she named me   Spanish girl.
I pretended I didn't speak it.
I pretended I didn't understand it.

The same way I pretended
I didn't care for cupcakes.

Childhood Transformation

When I was ten I sprouted wings. The dark pulse
of dread loomed in the hollow of my smallest self.
I found refuge under the tree of forty fruit, a multi-
blossom hybrid with showy tones of pink.

Slowly the skin on my arms developed follicles.
Feathers rose from tiny pits. Odd sensations
tingled & itched my shoulders & back.
My arms became wings, human & bird bound.

My mother bought me a cuttlebone
& mineral block for my chewing instinct. Friends
left seeds, suet cakes & tiny insects at my door.
My feathers molting, mother took me to a shaman.

Some had cast a *mal de ojo* on me. He ordered
me away from wide spaces & twisted
Joshua trees. He said, *this evil eye has pitched*
negative around her. Position a glass

of water behind every door & a small
mirror sewn into her skirt to reflect back
bad energy, absorb evil hounding her.
If not, she may disappear into the sunset

or plummet like a shattered bird of clay.
I molted one last time, the tree of forty fruit
sheltering me. A year later I began nibbling
on milkweed. I ate & ate to quell the new

rooting in my ribcage. Green fuzzed
my face & arms. I sprouted new
wings. Throbbing wings cleaving
to the light of my darkest wounds.

Grief Stopped By Today

She was traveling incognito.
She snuck up from behind & fixed
her hands around my throat. At once,

I offered to put on a pot of tea. She passed.
She waits at the circumference of my life.
I refuse to whittle a hollow in my heart.

Her prize: a sledgehammer of stone. A tin casket
of blackened bone. Years ago grief stalked
my sister-in-law. The prey, her daughter—

seven winters old, frozen with chemo, transplants,
life support until her name was poured back into the stars.
Today grief's smile stretches the borderland.

I watch a woman on Super Soul Sunday tell Oprah
how she lost three daughters to a Christmas fire.
Broken-winged hummingbirds blaze the room.

Grief scratches my hands, burns the marrow
in my bones. Talons once cloaked, rise in her eyes.
Do you hear the church bells ringing? I ask her.

Go quickly. The mourning parishioners
tire of thumbing rosary beads. They wait
to be led to a grave holed in glory.

I bolt my body against the night.
The chamomile tea over-steeped in bitters.
It warms my thimbled throat.

A Calla Lily for Maria

If you sign here, no mas dolor, it takes away
the pain, if you don't, your baby might die, Maria says
on the PBS documentary, describing the coercion
at the LA County hospital in the seventies.
Women went in to have babies & left sterilized.

Afterwards, the night sky scatters grieving women
denied the human right to bear a child.
They are dusted in despair. The seeds of bloom
are shattered across the American landscape.

In my dream, Maria sits at the river's edge.
Her baby has sprouted calla lilies on its head.
She snaps one off, uses its turgid spike to sweep
the bottom of the riverbank for dried up eggs.

Her starved *alma* drinks the yolks to slake its thirst,
refilling what's been pillaged from her body.
A shooting star burns the sky with silver rain.

Her case was brought to trial, long overdue.
The bloodless judge proclaimed,
the cultural background of these women
contributed to the problem.

I scream at the news, I slap the choking air,
his words, venom, spewing from a headless snake.
I channel Maria's stomping foot nailing him down.

Does our language, color or background make us
less valuable, Maria? No, *alma.* They had no right.

The calla lily stands for resurrection. We can blossom
once again with grace bearing any sterile depth.

The Droning River

Then you looked into the burdened sky,
a voice calling your name, a release
into the arms of the river,
the altar assuaging your sorrow.

The morning after, at the workplace,
a dissonant choir, co-workers broken
words, sounded in crescendo,
like the droning of cicada in July.

The newspapers reported they found you
in the river, a newborn nearby
in a garbage bag. Your god, rendered
helpless, grieved. His will undone.

We read Cisneros in a writing class.
You loved her Salvador: *the boy with eyes*
the color of caterpillar who is no one's friend.
A connected moment pillowed in marrow.

Sometimes I drive over the bridge.
Beneath it, haunted water,
the gateway that claimed you.
Whispering, *why*, my throat fastens.

I have known sorrow sated,
dragging me down to my knees
& I have known faith, this body's engine,
a clarity curling forth, to pull darkness out.

The cicada's song rises & falls in crescendo.
It sheds its shell before taking flight.

I Don't Tell My Son I Petition Mother Mary

We live like the ocean   moving
toward its desired direction in the dark.

In another life I was a whelk   carved in stone
my name was stitched to the sea.

In this life my son dreams
of being chased by black shoes.

Somewhere in the deep nadir
I can't reach him.

Why are we so afraid to be luminous?
Son, wherever you walk

your name is heard
in wide-open wind.

I don't tell him I chant prayer backwards
waging spiritual war for him.

I don't tell him faith unbraids fear
when my knees are knocking the floor.

I don't tell my son
I petition Mary   queen mother

to unbutton knots of darkness
lodged in his light.

What is a mother but an ocean
holding two beating hearts

one breaking—
          in waves.

Stone Turned Sand

I kiss the orchid petals
on the kitchen counter.

Whisper a secret into the plant.
I kiss a picture of my sons.
My framed world.

I once carried a fetus
for ten weeks four days two hours.
Prayed for a girl.

I carried her: a fabergé egg
of guilloché enamel.
Body dawning song.

I touch the lip of the orchid,
a landing platform for insects.

I am a quiet plea of honey bee.
Each weight-bearing wing

carrying stone
         turned sand.

Amends

Those last moments,
a bruised bird fluttered
around your death bed
waiting to be free.

You, father I never understood,
leave an ache,
spilling into empty arms,
one I must tend to over time.

Your last labored breath,
in the O of your mouth
is a sparrow of sorrow,
trilling into an empty sky.

We cleaned out your apartment.
I learned you stored long grain rice
in a yellow plastic container.
I claimed it as a keepsake,
a reliquary for holding the sacred,
keys & certificates: birth and death.

For years the relic sat on a pantry shelf
alive in its den of darkness,
spawning morsels of memories
like your hand, a flaming scarlet bird
lashing fear, striking, striking.

Inspired by Clementia,
the Roman goddess of mercy,
I soaked the container in forgiveness,
sudsed it in prayerful litany, chanting
our father, my father, non-father.

What I'm saying is—
it was time to expel the demons.

Grandmother's Fire Dance

Absence turned emptiness   in his ribs
just seven years old
when my father's mother died

How could he know   there were
so many ways   a moon could eclipse
the sound in your throat

He kept her picture in his pocket
a face caged in story
eyes slate gray   yearning

Abuela, I never knew—
I press her picture   to my cheek
a moth   ghosts my skin

Longing is a mottled field of spring
swallowing desire

In dreams we dance on the riverbed
Abuela kicks up her heels
split red pomegranates

She feeds me fire   I swallow flames
fearless in muscle & skin
my shadow burns   smolders   curls

Morning unspools a luminous sky
something worth naming
blooms beautiful

What is a wound but a fire
kindled & fed

Ghosted Album

1

Father, I am waiting here at the church
adorned in magnolia blossoms & dressed
in my divorced sister's gown.

The gods have granted my chance.
Hope you'll be here soon.

I imagine a drum roll
will announce your arrival.
In a father-of-the-bride-tux

you'll hold promises, apologies
& alibis, close to the vest,
of why you're not on time.

Your jacket will carry the scent
of Old Spice & Lucky Strikes,
the ones without the filter.

A friend once told me, *my dad cried
when he saw me in my wedding dress.*
Look how the tongue eclipses the heart.

2

Father, you reach me from the dead.
Hands ablated in burning regret.
Look how the wind carries remorse.

Isn't a father supposed to mine
the muscle of a daughter's heart?

I'll tell you about forgiveness—
I say I do on days I don't.
Yet still, you ghost my wedding album.

The Date

Years ago, my mother told me
mija, if you wear makeup to bed
when death comes knocking,
you'll be ready for the date.

I phone her. No answer.
Outside my window, the last
of yellow butter dahlia planted
stand undimmed.

I drive to her house
against wind whirring its lament.
The grey of day rubs
pencil lead across the sky.

On the road, a window display
of stiff mannequins posing
through a bare canvas stare,
vacant-eyed, in little black dresses.

A sudden longing for café con leche
made with large dollops of milk and sugar,
her color, warm. My need right now.

Hands shaking, I open the door.
Silence smothers me.
I begin to bargain with the universe,
I can be a better daughter.

Her face is loose and make-up free,
unadorned, fixed in a final blank.
She was wrong. So wrong.
A fist catches in my throat.

Elegy for the Other Side

Mama, you speak to me from the other side
4-32, the month & year you were born,

flashing on clocks, phones & license plates
in the thinning veil where the dream divides.

Voiceless you sing to me
the mouth of wind embroidered in song.

Before I was born I watched from the other side
& tried to help you transform your story.

Through moon-glazed dreams I cast shadows of a man,
wood-mouthed, who ate seeds & spit them into stones.

Once he fed you bruised buttercups
crushed in a blood-stained goblet.

Ruin is a felled bird in broken light,
a heart-skin hemorrhage.

The body is long, holds memory's song
stitched in the ladder of bone.

Mama, don't you know? I drink you up
like a cup of sun. I carry you wherever I go.

A Woman's Shape

When spirit becomes heavy it turns to water— Carl Jung

When I am afraid
I inhale water.
My tongue is bathed
in birdsong.
A woman who
breathes in water
chisels in light.
At times, I despair
I've fallen from grace.
Fear roots thick
under shadows.
I've used wounds
as a weapon. Wood
& stone as my shield.
Outside the petrichor
of summer's first rain
salves my soul. In the end
what will I regret?
When dawn blinks
I will be a postscript.
A woman like water
shapes the sea.

Elegy for a Mother Who Died Alone

Even the sun
blackened
the day I found you.

Even Antares—
giant red star
dimmed the night sky.

Through the window
sparrows fluttered past the lawn
gathering twigs, moss, feathers

for their nests   while I circled
the house of grief
in shallow breath.

You   who I carried
in the muscle of my mouth
should know:

morning breaks in empty hands.
I spit seeds & demand
into a crestfallen sky:

Mother, where are you?
If you're somewhere
between earth & abyss

reach this way. Come find me.
I've engraved your star
in the safe of my heart.

Pink Is Now a Color in the Rainbow

In the new world my eyes are pink
& my name is King.

Peonies sized as teacups
root in my mouth. I burrow

in terra firme. Tree-like. Some days oak.
Others more maple & woody.

I am resolved. An image pixilated, enlarged.
I speak le langage de fleurs: phlox, hockleaf

noon-head clocks. Their meanings hidden
to soften hard places. I am stippled light,

iron latticework. No war exists anywhere.
Everywhere is the dust of color & tremor.

We defer
        to the God of Rainbows.

In the new world we choose our words:
roses, flamingo, cherry blossoms, conch.

In the new world weeds thirst
for the color of voices—

blooming to be heard.

After Heavy Rains

In one hand the therapist holds a coke can.
Cradles it in the palm of the other.

Tell me something about your childhood.
I tell her about that time. I was nine.

Mother crouched in a window frame. Ready—
to jump. Her heart a shattered five & dime trinket.

Really? The therapist swings up her legs.
Criss-crosses them on the tired leather chair.

Go on, a quick swig of Coke quenches her thirst,
drains the air. She settles in like hard pelting rain.

My childhood spills on the floor.
Relay races its secrets to the door.

Outside a monsoon pummels the window.
I storyboard darkness. Scatter in air like threshed straw.

Sadness, my child-rooted friend, takes my hand.
She plucks out the goldcrest nesting in my hair.

Open, she says & mines underground my throat.
Go on, Go on, she whispers, Stand in the light.

Be pink like lilies—
                lifted after heavy rains.

Hunger-Song

Mother was found
dead   in bed

wearing Revlon Red Velvet
shade thirty-two.

On the radio Nina Simone
sang *Everything Must Change.*

Nothing stays the same
cause that's the way of time.

Spring is here again.
The crocus   blooms first

a show-off
in purples & yellows.

I am sluggish river
meandering in lack.

Morning brings sparrow's
hunger-song   hoisting

the fog in my head. His language holy,
echoing the native song in myself.

My heart-sore   lifts—
swells luminous   swells lodestar.

The Universe Has My Back

I divide my shipwrecks by smooth sailing in thin-skin.
I clot into the new normal. My secrets have secrets.
My secrets have needs. I hold onto them like
the strongest word in the human language—
a person's name. *Si Dios quiere,* my mother always said.
What does God will, anyway? Mondays, I talk to the universe—
the first hour is free. She says she has my back. She says
I'm too much work. I free range. Some days my body bleeds
in overtones of winter cabbage. Some days I'm left holding
the music of Mama's name, my son's first haircut clippings.
Too much pining wrestles the throat. I cut my not enough
in vinegar. Riddle it out of my ribs. Oh, how the body nails grief.
Oh, how the soul hammers for peace. I learn to sweet spot
in prayer. Jelly in gratitude. Lunar under a blue moon.

Silk on My Lap

Those days, need,
rattled my ribcage
      rearranging my spine.

A man once held me
      dusk till dawn.
His arms a life jacket

all night long.
      He asked for nothing.
The moon, jealous,

eclipsed blood orange.
      I once left my husband
for an hour. Phoned him

crying from a Hilton
      in a room painted,
Benjamin Moore, Lost-at Sea.

These days, need,
      is small, a silent room.
The moon spins silk on my lap.

Unraveling Knots

After Mama died   I unraveled
the hem of one of her blouses

sewing a dress
for my granddaughter

an invisible thread
to re-stitch her back to life

for years during holidays   Mama feigned
headaches toothaches stomach aches

claiming *nobody really cares*
what ailed Mama

knotting tufts of sadness
with each grief she held

I carry her disquiet
stitched in my blueprint

Mama teach me   how
to untie knots

without   unraveling myself

Louisa **Muniz** was born and raised in Perth Amboy, New Jersey. A former K-4 literacy coach and reading specialist, she was a National Board Certified teacher. She is the Sheila-Na-Gig 2019 Spring Contest Winner for her poem Stone Turned Sand. Her work has been nominated for Best of the Net and has appeared in *Tinderbox Journal, Menacing Hedge, Poetry Quarterly, PANK Magazine, Words Dance, Magnolia Review, Jelly Bucket,* among others. This is her first chapbook. She holds a MA from Kean University in Curriculum and Instruction. Louisa lives in Sayreville, NJ, with her husband.

CPSIA information can be obtained
at www.ICGtesting.com
Printed in the USA
LVHW090556090121
675851LV00006BA/533